The 2014 Poetry Marathon Anthology

Authors Publish Press
Bow, Washington

All rights reserved. No part of this book may be reproduced, stored in a retrieval system, or transmitted in any form or by any means, except as expressly permitted by the respective copyright holders.

The copyright for all poems in this book remains with the authors.

For more information, contact: support@authorspublish.com
Or visit: http://www.thepoetrymarathon.com

The Poets

HALF MARATHON 5

Adri Sinclair	10
Aisha Nazir	20
Britton Gildersleeve	7
Davita Joie	11
Donna Jean Siegel	23
George Saba	21
Harvey Schwartz	9
Ingrid Exner	19
Jennifer Faylor	14
Jennifer Spalding	13
Jessica Ankeny	22
Kat Eliza	17
Laura Kayne	16
Monica McCawley	24
Rhyana Juutilainen	15
Roxann Harvey	18

MARATHON 25

A.J. Edwards	29
Alora Wogsland	38
Angel Rosen	27
Anne McMaster	33
Bia Riaz	50
Caitlin Thomson	44

Carolyn Robinson	49
Cindy Albers	60
Denise Anderson	34
Ebony Larijani	47
Erin Hanson	32
Frida Mehtala	39
Hannah Frank	30
Hardika Sharma	59
Heather Stevens	46
Jaber Whacky	31
Jacob Jans	52
Jade Walker	54
JC Sullivan	43
Jennifer K. Lomax	42
Jessica Cruz	53
Joyce L. Bugbee	40
Meg Dunn	58
Mel Neet	55
Michellia D. Wilson	48
Nicole Rhea	36
Sally Hawker	41
Sara Khayat	56
Seema Sahoo	35
Shyami Nazzaro	57
Silvester Phua	51
Veronica Robbins	45
Virginia Carraway Stark	28
Wendy Hart	37

Introduction

On August 23rd 2014, poets and writers from around the world got up at odd hours and stayed up for 12 or 24 hours. During that period of time they wrote a poem every hour and published it within that hour on the official website.

A very quick turn around and a very exhausting day. But many things were written and many boundaries were broken. A poet who had not written in a decade managed to write 24 poems in one day. Other poets found themselves writing about unusual or unexpected things.

When I first came up with this idea, the idea to write 24 poems in 24 hours, I imagined doing it alone. I thought few people would understand the idea and fewer would want to try it.

But when I told my husband, Jacob Jans, about it three years ago he wanted to try it too and we wrangled in a few friends. It was a fun and productive event, but we could never imagine very many people participating.

This year however a hundred people attempted the whole or half marathon and at least 50 completed one or the other. These people were in England, in India, in Sweden, in Africa, in Lebanon, in the US and Canada, and in many other countries.

This Anthology includes one poem by everyone who completed the half or full marathon and submitted their poems for inclusion in this anthology.

The participants were strangers before the day, but from it a community formed, out of staying up late, out of writing like crazy, and out of encouraging one another not to give up, even when the power went out or a storm happened.

I am so impressed by these poets, by the work they produced, and the community they created.

Caitlin Jans (Thomson)

Half Marathon Poems

Britton Gildersleeve

Hive Structure
___

i.
My nieces bring me bees.
Strung on copper, hung from chains.
Each as different as my nieces
who do not understand their own faces

i..
While the bees   who dance in darkness
can map for any sister
the way home. Can fly on wings
stronger than maps.

iii.
My nieces build themselves homes.
With a lover, a husband, a wife.
Each love as different as my nieces.
Spring and summer, autumn honeys.

iv.
My nieces drink the tea I brew for them
in cups that were my mother's
that fit on saucers my grandmother painted.
So many women.

v.
I drop honey from a silver spindle
trail it like the scent of roses
beneath bee flight. All the bees are sisters.

vi.
My nieces breathe in harmony.
Their dances filled with light
the light filled with wings. The bees
work in the late summer
while my nieces inhale   exhale.

vii.
In the late afternoon, my nieces
ready for leave-taking. Fill sacks
with food I baked for them,
as if propolis was held within.

viii.
My nieces' wings are music.
Each composes her own melody
She turns and spins within

Harvey Schwartz

Pinocchio Loves Pistachios

But when he eats them
his nose grows long.
And though he fights
his appetite
his nose grows longer,
he's not contrite.

Geppetto cries
inside a whale.
But a tickling feather
saves the day.

What we learn
from fairy-tales
is known to us
beyond life's veils.

Don't eat pistachios.
Stay out of whales.
And there are fairies
everywhere.

Adri Sinclair

Word Assassination

There is thunder in my head,
a storm brewing silently,
big words are floating free,
assassin's variety.
Pencil, pen, paint?
Pick your poison, I'll write the suicide note,
Grammatically correct, a saga or a novelette?
The thunder rubs into lightning,
the storm pass by quietly,
smaller words captured perfectly,
assassin's sobriety.

Davita Joie

The Healer

for Zion

"Does it hurt?" she asks

Tracing the bumpy protrusion on my upper chest
With all the tenderness her
Two-year-old finger can muster
Furrowed brow

"Not anymore," I say
"It's all healed."

I lie.

I don't say that
Sometimes I lie in bed
Awakened by its renewed
Throbbing

That healed things on the outside are often
Unhealed in places we can't see
Pulsing with
Resentment at having been
Violated in the first place

A desire resurfaces
Restates its original objection
Brings the pain out of the shadows for a
Reunion

Hi
Remember me?

I don't say
There are new wounds
Birthed in this place, named
Raw and Open and were she to
Touch them, no matter how tenderly
The pain would be excruciating

No scab
No scar

Just the sting of shred nerves, the
Aching of verbal lashes, salt ladled
With cruel, liberal hands
Languishing untended on the
Battlefield

I don't say
Time enough for the Reality of
Things Healed Over
When she is old

"All better," she says
Not a question

I tear
Wish her tenderness would last forever
In the tip of her tracing, trusting finger
She has the power to
Heal

Jennifer Spalding

A Maddening Love

What can I say?
What may I do for you?
Name it, it is yours.
For I am no more than a slave,
A tramp, a handmaiden, a lover,
A whore, a bitch, a mother, a friend, and a soul mate.
Whatever you want me to be.
However, I can no longer stand the slander.
Each word uttered tears at my heart,
Rips me to pieces.
Realization whips me across the face,
Something is amiss.
Memories whiz through my mind,
Too many drugs,
Addiction, affliction,
Twisted, tainted,
Slanted, and warped.
It dawns on me how utterly hopeless this all is.
I am all you said and much more.

Jennifer Faylor

The Hermit

I read a news article about a hermit in the woods
that has finally been captured, after decades
of stealing his necessities from nearby homes.

27 years in this forest in Maine, and never once
saw a doctor, never once got sick.
"You have to have contact with other humans
in order to get sick," he says.

It breaks my heart to think that this might be true.
Why would human beings be created in such a way
that their destruction only came
from being nearer to each other?

Continuing the article, my heart stops again
as I read that he's not used to other people's faces,
so the hermit avoids eye contact,
"there's too much information there," he explains.

And I think of the man I love,
and how he couldn't raise his eyes to meet mine,
the day I said that I was leaving him.

Rhyana Juutilainen

My Lover

My head rests on your shoulder.
Your hand rubs my back to comfort.
I touch the recent mark
that the comforting hand made.
I should run away from the monster
but who else will love me
with all the marks on my body?

Laura Kayne

Not Tea

I'm English, we solve everything with a cup of tea,
I joke with a smirk as I pick up my drink.
I breathe it in, and then frown a little,
For this drink is not my tea.

Darker, stronger, but just as hot,
Pungent smell and aftertaste.
This I have tasted before –
But this is not my tea.

Another breakfast drink,
Not English by a long shot.
Full of flavour, energizing for the day,
But not always my cup of tea.

Kat Eliza

New

Maybe the joy of meeting someone new
Trumped all my precautions
And maybe getting addicted to you
Was not the healthiest of my options

Roxann Harvey

Summer Time

When I think of you
My heart melts like butter....
You beam so bright!
It's so great to see your beauty
Lay in the sun
Feel the gentle breeze
Enjoy the sand and sea
Basking in your leisure
Is such a wonderful blessing to me!

Ingrid Exner

Dear Emily-

Thank you for your words today
written centuries ago.
Their wisdom has more meaning
than ever you would know.

Wise words that you provide
take flight from my page.
Resting in imagination, they strive
to leave remembrances-
Alive!

Hope, Freedom, Pain and Release-
YOU address them all.
With metaphors that will not cease
and similes that sing sweet song,
leading readers now to peace.

Aisha Nazir

Beauty is Sumptuous

Beauty is sumptuous, riders of uncertainty
Truth is no certainty, you who hold on to reality
War is not irrefutable, givers of reason
You wonder why be reasonable, in oceans of treason?
Fights are necessary, dreamers of amnesty
Yet blessed with reason peaceful, do not receive cruelty
Peace is the courage, priests of satisfactions
Are as they as satisfying, holy transactions?
Fear is ever worshipped, guardians of the faithful
Dare not play with faith since it is job of the fearful
Words are for meanings, listeners of perception
Though it has been perceived they give poor reception
Forgiveness is so vast, regiment of mercy
For each merciless soul demanding decree
Truth is merely a decision, collectors of wisdom solemn
Between truth and notional apprehension common
And they say, beauty is sumptuous, riders of uncertainty
For happiness maybe peace in misery.

George Saba

Yours Truly

Ignite me with the flames
Of your heart
Burn me down to ashes
And blow them away
Let me travel the world
See unexplored lands

Then imprison me in the jar
Of your thoughts
And never open the lid
Take safety measures
Never let that jar break
Never let anything harm it

I will forever be yours
And you will forever possess me

Jessica Ankeny

Hour 12

Water wraps the boat
around the bottom. Wraps
the dock and wooden stops.
Rubs against them. Up and
down. Up and down. Across.
Justin comes. Knows something
is wrong. Doesn't ask
and stands close enough that we
are always touching. Tells me
about poetry. About Starbucks.
About boys and sunscreen.
I will not remember why
the world had turned
to mist, but I remember
why it came back.

Donna Jean Siegel

Haiku

Death is not darkness.
It is the worlds I travel
At night in some dreams.

Monica McCawley

My Morning Love

My morning dates with you
Sometimes last all day long;
As I smell your tasty aroma
I can't help but burst out in song.
Please don't ever leave me!
I need you by my side;
You're there when I am tired
You're there when I write.
I love you, my friend
And as I start another poem;
I can't help but be reminded
To make sure your power's on.

Marathon Poems

Angel Rosen

Add-or-exic

she was a straight-C math student
who hated graphing fractions,
in a flood of A's and extracurricular
until she started skipping
lunch
the excuse sounded something like
the half an hour to do homework
was more mandatory
than the menu
in two months she brought her
math grade up ten percent and dropped
ten percent of something else,
the way she was
learning to divide her body
made her understand why she had to find "x"
each meal taught her to add
and she invented new ways to subtract
in five months she
became the fraction
and the only thing on the graph
was two digit numbers
and red circles to mark
every
wrong
answer.

Virginia Carraway Stark

Her Face

Her face looked gaunt and old

her body bloated more

each time I saw her

she thought she could block up the
door

with a pendant of the goddess
of disappointment

entwined around her neck

on a silver chain rich with tarnish

divorce and disappointment clotted every doorjamb

she was only so angry

because nobody loved her anymore

I don't live with her

Like ivy my love puts fingers into every crack

that her despair left behind
I would rather tear the structure down

than to live with her old corpses

anymore.

A.J. Edwards

Sweatpants

The fat lazy woman in sweatpants
Complaining she's fat
Blaming motherhood for that
While eating a Snickers

That's who I called mom
She called her dad
Whenever anything ever
Went even slightly wrong

I learned little from her
Except, maybe, what not to do
To be a strong grown woman
I mustn't be like you, Mom

Hannah Frank

Not Mine

Arms wrap around your middle,
lips caress your neck.
Whispers turn your hair erect.
You melt into a soft body
and hands run up your back,
but they're not mine,
not anymore.

Jaber Whacky

dryad
---

she is elfin – its in her eyes;

the tourmaline tinged satyr,
that mischievously shies

in numinous splendor; she peers
through the canvas of the night –

head to toe, covered in tenebrous delight.

Erin Hanson

Cinderella

Dust and rags and broomsticks,
She would wash and scrub and clean,
Under the wrath of two step sisters,
Who found joy in being mean,
And a plump fairy godmother,
With a crack upon her wand,
Dooming every spell she ever cast,
To go completely wrong,
A ball gown turned to tatters,
Two glass slippers turned to boots,
Out of place among the dresses,
And the gold embroidered suits,
She ran as time struck midnight,
Worried what else could go wrong,
Didn't lose a single thing,
Her boots stayed firmly on,
So she ran and ran still further,
Until the sunlight filled the sky,
Not even pausing briefly,
To wave that horrid life goodbye,
She broke free from their judgment,
And hasn't cared to look back since,
She doesn't need their greedy longing,
And she doesn't need a prince.

Anne McMaster

Memento Mori

I kept my mother's work clothes when she died.
The farming ones she wore through sun and rain.

And dreamed - as children hope and adults never do –
That she'd come back to wear them once again.

Denise Anderson

Prayers on Water

She wakes to meet the day
While slumber has a hold on others.

She rides the waves of silence
Soft, soft silence
Falls into her hands
Like catching snowflakes
In winter.

Rocking in the waves
The rhythm of the water
Is her own.

Listen
She will tell you
What there is to know.

She is the waves,
The waves are her,
And they are ONE.

Seema Sahoo

Clinging Mind

Thunderstorm cascade
From unending darkness
Irrational fear clasps
The clinging mind..

Nicole Rhea

Silence

I am forgetting your voice.
I don't have it captured anywhere.
I kick myself for that
All this technology
Buzzing
Brain melting stuff
and I never thought to record your voice
I remember my aunt used to record Christmases when we were little
I want to comb through the pile of tapes and find you
Hold you again
If only with my ears.
I could close my eyes and hear your voice
Run my hand down the path you always ran down my cheek
Pretend it was you there
Comforting me like you would have
Pretend it was your thumb on my cheek and not my own.
When I could curl up at your feet and put my head in your lap, forever 10 years old.
How do I do these things without you?
Get married?
Have babies?
Who am I going to call for help when the baby wont stop crying?
How can I be a mother...
Without mine to show me how???

I run my thumb down my tear stained face.
Pretend its yours again.
Try and hear you.
Silence.

Wendy Hart

The Choice

At a crossroads, there she stood;
Confused and all too weary;
One road evil, one was good;
She could not help be teary.

Which to choose, she did not know;
Her mind was in bundle;
Good was right, bad was sorrow;
One would be so dull.

She hungered for danger, action and fun;
The fast lane was inviting;
But deep inside her decision was done;
It was to be exciting.

She knew she had to take the good;
No other way would do;
She was assured that she could;
Begin to start anew.

So straight ahead her path was drawn;
The answer was so clear;
Onward marching, toward the dawn;
So sure and without fear.

Alora Wogsland

Anxiety Attack

hands twitch,
mind races,
stomach curls,

fingers rake through hair,
breaths come quick,
thoughts race,

arms curl around legs,
body rocks,
forward and back.

forward and back.
a burst of terror,
breath stops.

movement stops.
completely frozen.
terror passes,

rocking starts again,
hands run along legs,
unable to stay still,

thoughts run in circles,
half-formed questions,
and irrational fears.

Frida Mehtala

Sacrilege

I spoke to him of gentle ways,
how one can treat it
almost like an illness.
The frenzy turmoil and hollow
insides,
as a joke between gods and humans.

Joyce L. Bugbee

Untitled

The pen in my hand
the clock on the wall
Can the pen write fast enough
before time passes
Ideas swarm in my head
words reach out
Some land on the page
others fly on by
When the right ones get together
a poem may be born

Sally Hawker

Yes

Yes, I must welcome this new winter of the world.
I've shunned her before and paid the price
In callous coldness- in a winter alone.
I can only hope that by my own emitting light, I can take away the internal chill that brings on your oblivion.
For warmth can be found in the coldest of winters, but this must start by welcoming in the night, to illuminate it later.

Jennifer K. Lomax

The Smile on My Face

There's a smile on my face,
I am happy it seems.
This smile can mean so many things.
It can hide the truth,
Though that's not a lie.....
There's more to me that meets the eye.
I am good at pretending,
At keeping it real.
Just because my face doesn't show it.....
Does it mean the pain is not real?
If I told you the truth of what goes through my mind.
The circus, the battle, the voices that cry.....
Sometimes I wish I could get away from me.

Oh such a peaceful place that would be.

JC Sullivan

No, my dog didn't eat my first poem...

my computer is functioning fine
and while I'd love to blame my not promptly posting on
wordpress,
that's not the truth, either.
I keep my promises. I don't promise often. Easier that way.
But
a chance to audition for Oscar-winning director Steve McQueen
is an opportunity that comes along maybe once every 12 years...
So I made a compromise.
I went uptown writing along the way. All the way to 145th street, to be exact.

The line snaked for several Manhattan-sized city blocks.
I stood out. No, it wasn't the poet glowing from within. Tho that didn't hurt.
I was the only blonde. One of three females.
A rep looks at me and says, "I'm sure you're very talented BUT I don't think
you could play an African-American male convincingly."
I smile.
Fair enough. But to audition for Steve McQueen...
"The notice said, ALL people welcome and I am a person."
We both grinned.
"Misprint." and seeing my disappointment added, "Unfortunately just males."
Do I trust him? Is he speaking the truth?
"We are accepting drop-offs." he encouraged me.
I look at the line meandering around the block and another block and another
block and still going...
Thanking him, I hand him my headshot and resume.

Today, my creative energy is better spent writing poetry.

Caitlin Thomson

Sound Carries Across The Bay

I have woken to gunshots a hundred times.
It is just hunting season, my husband
reassures me, as they become our alarm clock.

I can't remember the first gun I saw,
in a movie surely, and then my great grandfather,
the war hero's gun. I was so young,
I didn't know what to say but pretty.

I know the first one I heard, sleeping
at a friend's house on New Years eve
we both commented on the sound, assumed
fireworks, till the next morning.

Ever since then I have known
the difference. I have never held
one myself, but I have told a hunter
where to shoot, and did not regret it.

Veronica Robbins

The Bering Sea

I don't know much about the Bering Sea
Except that it's cold
Deep
Dangerous
Everything I know is from television
Fishermen turned TV stars
Everyday men doing deadly work
Weather that drives it all

Everything I know is from television
Except that you're there
At night I think of you and
I can feel the cold wind
And see the white crests of waves
Washing over the deck
As young men struggle to hold on
And pull lines of fish aboard,
Their focus split between life and livelihood

I whisper your name
Say a prayer
Push away the fear
Send you my love

And wish I didn't know anything about the Bering Sea

Heather Stevens

Shed

Pretty as can be, I feel sorry for her.
While the physical seems in tact,
her emotional is dry and lack.

With each man, she bids farewell to another piece of herself.
Never really touching life, just watching from a dusty shelf.

Fed up with each violation,
just not enough to salvage what's left of her next generation.

I pray she finds a new revelation.
One she can hang her hat on, trust with no questions.
Let sleeping dogs lie, finally learn her lesson.

Realization, that who she is at the break of wake is by itself, a beautiful blessing.
Rise up!
Break away, and start your shedding.

Ebony Larijani

Tug Less The War...

The under toe, on my tippy toes, yoga, less the tug, my body left the war

Michellia D. Wilson

The Raging and Consuming War of the Poetics

Part XXI

October,
the month when the monsters
begin to haunt,
drift inside the attic of my body,
the trunk with all these memories,
rattles, begging me to stir up trouble,
I oblige and I soon find myself
in the asylum.

Carolyn Robinson

poem for the language angel

come sweet language angel,
i am the red sister
consuming love like fire-
honey falling over delicious dirt-
put in the universe to grow you.-
overwhelm you with emotion and words.
come sweet language angel
dance the light of heaven-
embrace an innocent neighbor-
woman, boy or girl-
fill their hands with music, beauty and art-
so each one can live happy and full.
come sweet language angel
with your delicious kiss,
go wild filling my universe with a thousand words-
never embracing old memories and pain-
only believing i will pronounce life
wherever i go.
come sweet language angel-
you with your supernal words and me with my mess-
blend us into a song of hope and light-
blend us into one sweet flower destined to live throughout
eternity.

Bia Riaz

Hushed and Haunted Rhythms

There is a certain nightly hour when an eerie hush cushions the earth.
All becomes dormant, all becomes quiet
Except
The little sounds thrive and grow and pulse and move and shake and quiver.
Close your eyes, turn off all the lights and listen to their stories.
The manic march of the wall clock; tick-tock, tick-tock
The determined deep vibrato of the refrigerator
The soft subtle "swooshing" of the ceiling fan; still on a focused mission to drive away the heat
But listen closer; go deeper within
Cup your hands to your ears
Beyond the heavy footsteps of your boldly beating heart, listen for the other rhythms.
The ones you usually ignore.
The cacophony of caffeine cruising through your veins at dangerously high speeds
The brawling beasts in your belly; escapees from a banned mosh-pit
Your long laboring lungs like violent waves crashing.
The longer you listen, the louder they become.
Harder to ignore
Sometimes sneaking into your waking world.

Silvester Phua

It's Eight, And Little Red's In The Hood

"Hey girl, where you going?"
Sun's hardly gone down,
And the wolves are out and about already.

"Stranger, Danger!" I remember.
Head down, look at the ground,
Make no eye contact, step away quickly.

But they circle me, taunting rapidly.
There's just no going forward,
No retreat back.

Unwanted hands move in to trespass.
I grimace, recoil, shun their attention.
"No, stop it," I glower.

They pull off my red scarf,
And I pull out my kukri,
Cutting, thrusting, slashing.

Twitching, they lie still; I hurry off,
And speed dial my ex-Gurkha grandfather:
"Sorry *baje*, I am on my way."

Jacob Jans

Sonnet for Hour Twenty

I want to be a hypochondriac.
The arrogance of it appeals to me.
The knowledge gained of what must surely be
my ills seems lovely. I'd like to stack
the cards in front of me and know their names.
I want my aches and pains to mean a lot.
I want to buy some drugs and know I've got
a fighting chance. And yes, I want to blame
myself for what I've done. Mistakes were made
that caused the cancer that might come, or has.
Who knows? Just run the test. I'm not some spaz.
The ache I feel is real and doesn't fade.
I want a name for it. Let's have a look.
I wonder if it's even in a book.

Jessica Cruz

Gathered in Thought

Something is about to happen,
I put so much in to writing a classic.
Stick to my guns of what I know is magic.
Emphasis on bad behavior and over dramatic.
Scenic photos of the East Coast and Mid-West tragic.
Metaphors are never real life accidents.
They keep us gathered in thought; rather than in action.

Jade Walker

Pick Me, Pick Me

Was it by dreaming or
Writing
That I could find out what I
Thought
Nightmares or strokes of a pen
Fairy dust or ink
Screams or words
Not fond of either
Does it matter
They both sired
Me

Mel Neet

Blue

Rivulets of blue light stream
onto the desk, itself a corpus of productive thought.
I watch myself in slow motion, missing the mark
and unable to pull back to the moment I could gain myself.
There are no night terrors,
only the satisfaction, suspended, of falling
onto a pillow and feeling my body's descent
as through clouds.
Energy to take up the gauntlet for art,
for poetry, for self-awareness
dissolves with each hour but I stay
until the light appears through
window blinds. Dawn.

Sara Khayat

ursula

there was an offensive seagull nesting below our balcony.
we watched the ocean with tired eyes as the seagull
attacked every person brave enough to get close.
we gave her a name and a home and we nested
there until we were ready to grow.
playing poker on a hotel pillow drinks at stake,
chemical gambles
betting a bottle on a colorful hand and now i see exactly what
i'm gambling on i knew nothing easy is good enough.
i gulped the night quickly to feel it hit harder.
the next day the seagull's beak warned us
we stepped too close to beauty.

Shyami Nazzaro

Oh, Just Trust

Oh, just trust.
Have I failed you yet?
You keep declaring it's the end of the story,
And yet, I know it isn't.
No wonder you are disappointed.
You have not gotten to the best part.
Stop truncating majesty.
Stop nailing down mystery.
You will see, once you are wide, wide open,
Why I first began your story at all.

Meg Dunn

Home is Where the Heart is

So often there is a sense
of feeling adrift, disconnected
An indescribable feeling of loneliness

A sense of a small battered vessel
Being thrown about in a choppy sea

Lamenting for a sheltered cove
the warmth of a fire side
the smell of a home cooked meal

The promise of a loving embrace
The feeling that sense of 'home'
We all yearn for the home of
our heart of hearts

Some find it immediately,
and grip it with both hands
never to leave their sight

For others it's a search,
Ongoing for some time
even for a life time.

Search and searching for the light
in the stormy seas
To that special place of where
the heart of heart lives
That place called Home.

Hardika Sharma

Way To Go

Say it whenever you can
tell someone who listen
See everything when you can
observe what appeals the most
Travel to the far land
Wander to find the unknown
Walk while going to work
Run to catch your dream
Do what makes you happy
but create what makes others smile

Cindy Albers

Too Many Poems

Prompt for hour who cares
Been doing this too long
Yes I profess to being a poet
But after 20 odd
I feel like a poser
A supposer
Passion?
Hell no
Poetry feels like poison now
I drank it
My stomach aches
My head bursts
How much coffee can one person drink?
Annoying and annotated
Sonnets and Free verse
To rhyme or not to rhyme
Can we just finish this thing?
I have to work in the morning
I'll be poetizing all day
Sleeping at the wheel
I'll be mortified
Mummified
Metered and alliterated
I'll be making haikus out of salami
Metaphors out of the cash register
Too many poems I tell you
Its gone on too long

Head exploding
Brain imploding
Too many blasted poems

www.ingramcontent.com/pod-product-compliance
Lightning Source LLC
Chambersburg PA
CBHW060506080526
44584CB00015B/1573